I0453776

Zelda's Bed spans 72 hours in Montgomery, Alabama.

Making a pilgrimage plagued by travel delays and extreme heat, Klecko spends an August weekend at the Scott and Zelda Fitzgerald Museum to launch *The Dead Fitzgeralds*, the first book in his Fitzgerald trilogy. Located in Montgomery's Cloverdale neighborhood, the museum is in a home where the couple lived briefly in 1931; it now shares space with an Airbnb.

For Klecko, a stranger in a strange land, being in the South is surreal and intriguing. A place where he thrives as he delivers his message about the Fitzgeralds. Once that mission is complete, he wanders to Hilltop where he does tarot readings for a line of people stretched out the door of a Montgomery nightclub into the summer heat. From there, he bides his time well into the night, a bottle of Crown Royal at his side, under a sprawling magnolia tree in the Fitzgeralds' front yard.

The mystery of Zelda Fitzgerald is revealed during a night he spends in her bedroom. And he discovers the sad charm of Zelda's love for her Montgomery hometown, and her dreams for the future as he trudges, parched and hungover, through Oakwood Cemetery on a Sunday morning.

In real time, it's hard to notice
Silence without exception
Leads up to
The crescendo of a moment

In 72 hours, Klecko experiences the moments of a lifetime and the kindness of strangers in a place called Montgomery, Alabama.

Praise for *3 a.m. Austin Texas*

Named one of the Ten Best Books of 2021 by *Superior Reads*

Longlisted for Best Independent Book of 2021 by *Shelf Unbound*

"Listen to the emotions and energy packed into Klecko's clearly expressed phrases."

Lone Star Literary Life

Praise for *Lincolnland*

"You should be very proud of this book, and the way you wrote it, living it out day by day, the world around you seen and formed by your imagination. Well done, my friend."

Leif Enger, author of
Peace Like a River and *Virgil Wander*

"Congrats, man! Enjoy every minute."

George Saunders, winner of the Man Booker Prize for
Lincoln in the Bardo

"Danny Klecko is an 'action poet' in the same way painters from the 1950s were action painters. He is always in motion, and unlike most of the rest of us, there is never a dull moment."

Thomas R. Smith, poet and author of *Medicine Year*
and 30-year private secretary to Robert Bly

"The thing about Danny Klecko is you either 'get' where he's coming from, or you don't . . . *Lincolnland* is deeply personal writing from all kinds of Klecko's experiences as he stood on spots where Lincoln stood."

Mary Ann Grossmann, St. Paul Pioneer Press

"Congratulations on your award . . . I am glad that you embraced your talent and calling and became a poet."

Sjón

"Klecko sounds great."

Jonathan Franzen

Praise for _Hitman-Baker-Casketmaker: Aftermath of an American's Clash with ICE_

Winner of the 2020 Midwest Book Award for General Poetry Notable 100: 2019 _Shelf Unbound_ Best Independent Book

"In Klecko's personal, powerful collection of poems, he grapples with his feelings on a variety of topics, including baseball, family and the fallout of a U.S. Immigration and Customs Enforcement Audit."

Tim Carman, Washington Post

"Danny Klecko is my hero for taking on ICE and writing radical poetry in the tradition of Robert Bly and Tom McGrath."

Mary Ann Grossmann, St. Paul Pioneer Press

"Klecko writes like Steinbeck on steroids."

Sue Zumberge, owner of SubText Books in
downtown St. Paul

"Klecko's affection and respect for his crew spill out onto the pages."

Lee Svitak Dean, *Star Tribune*

"Klecko cuts a memorable figure. He's tall and has been known to train in a boxing gym. An impressive array of tattoos covers his arms and legs. Klecko says he doesn't have the answers, but people need to talk about who is providing their daily bread."

Euan Kerr, Minnesota Public Radio

"This is a memorable collection. These are Henry Miller poems in a rough language that makes even Frank O'Hara seem delicate and lyrical."

Joel Van Valin, editor of *Whistling Shade*

"Illegal immigrants can't bother with renown. At least, not the kind that a Paris-destined baker, or a poet, or a novelist might chase. And yet, in *Hitman*, Klecko finds it most fitting to immortalize the moments and people who typically go unsung."

Erik Tormoen, *Minnesota Monthly*

"Klecko probably doesn't look like the first guy you'd expect to write a book of verse probing our national immigration question from a first-hand perspective."

Drew Wood, *Mpls. St. Paul Magazine*

"Klecko – a baker who writes poems. A friend with integrity. A loyal human being. An award-winning author. This is so fucking good."

David Fhima, world-renowned chef

"People in the industry know that bakers tend to be a spiritual lot. One of our most philosophical has to be the St. Paul baker that goes by one name: Klecko. He's written for years about the industry and baking life for different publications, but his new work is very personal, and important."

Stephanie March, *Mpls. St. Paul Magazine*

Other books by Klecko

The Dead Fitzgeralds

3 a.m. Austin Texas

Lincolnland

Hitman-Baker-Casketmaker: Aftermath of an American's Clash with ICE

Out for a Lark

The Bluebeard of Happiness

A Pox Upon Your Blessings

Houdini in St. Paul

My British Hindu Bible

Robert Bly and the Monk in His Cell

Mayor 4 Life

Brando Land

ZELDA'S BED

Published in 2023 by Paris Morning Publications

www.parismorningpublications.com

Copyright © Paris Morning Publications

All rights reserved. No part of this book may be used or reproduced without written permission from the publisher, except in the case of brief quotations embodied in critical articles and reviews.

Published and reprinted in the United States of America

ISBN: 979-8-218-13231-6

Cover design by Audrey Campbell

ZELDA'S BED

BY KLECKO

PARIS MORNING
PUBLICATIONS

To Lori Greenberg for her vision
To the North Asheville Library and to Battery Park Book
Exchange & Champagne Bar for their hospitality
To the good people of Asheville for never forgetting Zelda
And with heartfelt gratitude to Therese Anne Fowler for
her generous advice and for being a pioneer by shining a
light on Zelda in her smash hit, Z: A Novel of
Zelda Fitzgerald

INTRODUCTION

My son, the St. Paul public school teacher
Told me book reports were no longer relevant
At the school where he was teaching
He told me the powers that be
Felt inner city high school students
Didn't possess the focus needed
To get through a novel
My son, the St. Paul public school teacher
Told me now books were summed up
With one paragraph
So, if you wanted to teach *The Great Gatsby*
If you wanted to dialogue with the class
About its content
The teacher had to pick
A single paragraph
That represents the author's work

My friend, the university professor
Had me come to her class
To read poems
And discuss poetry
With students
In her freshman English course
My friend, the university professor
Told me that once these students
Completed her course
Half of them
Would never read a novel
During the remainder of their lives

Books have made me confident
Books have made me c ever
When I think of an entire generation
Or even a substantial fraction
Of a generation
More interested in devices
Than pages, columns and novels
I shudder to consider the future
Their future
Because I'm pretty certain
I can determine the outcome

Just in my state alone (Minnesota)
I have seen enrollment in classic scholarship groups
Dwindle
Look at Sinclair Lewis
Look at F. Scott Fitzgerald
Their message doesn't seem as relevant
How can it be
When it's not plugged into
Today's ever-changing world

Listen up
Post middle-aged baby boomers
If we don't find a way
To connect our past
To the next generation's future
Toni Morrison
Ernest Hemingway
Sylvia Plath
Alex Haley
Jack Kerouac
James Baldwin
Joan Didion
And Eve Babitz
They'll all vanish

I thought about this
For some time
With uncertainty
With apprehension
Until
I came to the conclusion
F. Scott Fitzgerald
Would be my primary tool
F. Scott Fitzgerald
Would be my ambassador
To the new world
But first I would have to
Ditch the antiquated vernacular
And replace it with colloquial slang

The first thing I did
Was to bring an author
AJ Odasso
Up from New Mexico
To present their book
The Pursued and the Pursuing
At the University Club
(A venue Scott & Zelda frequented)
In front of the most openly gay crowd
The U Club has ever seen

In AJ's novel
Jay Gatsby gets shot, but lives
And falls in love with Nick Carraway
As the two go off to rebuild a new life
Daisy Buchanan resurfaces
And pleads with Gatsby
To mentor her daughter
Pam Buchanan
Who happens to be queer

When I first pitched this show
On social media
The program received mixed reactions
Many people were supportive
And complimented the fresh take
While others claimed the queer angle
Was nothing short of heresy
However . . .
The end result was a full house
Most of which was made up
Of members of the LGBTQ community
AJ Odasso's book
Not only brought these folks
Closer to her characters
But to Fitzgerald's as well

After witnessing this success
I wrote a book entitled
The Dead Fitzgeralds
With an understanding
That if I wanted to be
Wiser than the serpent
I would write a plotline
That trended heavy
With a metaphysical demographic
I also made certain
To make certain this book
Was soaked in St. Paul lore
When most books are written
About anything to do with Fitzgerald
They always seem to be weighted down
With scholarship and footnotes
Today's youth could care less
That's why I filled my book
With gossip

The conclusion to my vision
Was to pitch a partnership proposal
To the St. Paul Public Libraries
I explained how I wanted to resurrect
Fitzgerald, and his short stories
While making them inclusive
So everyone would feel welcomed
The St. Paul Public Libraries
Agreed, and therefore
I shall always remain grateful

THE BOOK LAUNCH

Rain
Publisher and I depart
Minneapolis to Montgomery, via Charlotte
Charlotte cancelled, DC instead
Anne Heche is dead
Boarding delayed
Salman Rushdie attacked
Take Off – Touch Down
Montgomery connection . . . missed
Fly to Birmingham, rent a car
Altercation at the Enterprise parking lot
Salman Rushdie stabbed in the liver
May lose an eye
Headlights, heat, cicadas, moonlight
Eagle Radio 106.9 – Sister Christian
Montgomery at midnight
Liquor store closed
919 Felder Avenue
The Fitzgerald Museum

ACCOMMODATIONS

I dropped my luggage in the Zelda Suite
Publisher is across the hall
In the F. Scott Suite
I look for a liquor cabinet
I look for a wine rack
Jesus – Mary – Joseph
Hummus, bananas and Coke Zero
Will have to co
Until I check my phone
And find there is a 24-Hour liquor store
Less than a mile away
This discovery is appealing
But that would mean
I'd have to ask the Publisher
To borrow the car keys
A glaring indicator that maybe I like booze
A little more than I'm supposed to
Instantly I'm saved by the thought
That the Publisher has probably already realized
I'm a functional alcoholic
By the grace of God, my pathetic condition
Dissipates within moments as I grew weary
The bananas weren't bad

FRIENDS

In the dining room, on the wall
Dozens of Zelda's childhood friends
Had their images displayed on placards
In the dining room, on the floor
Were two placards, underneath a table
The one on the top
I didn't know
But the one on the bottom
KABOOM
It was Tallulah Bankhead

FRIENDS

Years ago, I saw a host
On Turner Classic Movies
Talk about her, before the movie
LIFEBOAT
The host explained
The entire film was shot
In a boat, in a pool
On a secure Hollywood set
The host explained
To reach the pool
The cast had to climb a ladder
When Tallulah climbed
It became apparent
She didn't wear panties
Complaints and more complaints
Were brought to Hitchcock
Who explained . . .
Talk to makeup, or hairdressing
This isn't my department

LIQUOR STORE RUN

At 5:35 a.m. I woke up
At 5:38 a.m. I realized I wasn't at home
Today would be the first time in my 59 years
That I would spend an entire day in Alabama
At 5:39 a.m. I picked up my phone
At 5 a.m. the Publisher sent me a text
Telling me to make my way over
To Fitzgerald Park when I was ready
Zip – Shower
Zip – Banana
Zip – Bang – Boom
At 5:59 a.m. I was reunited with the Publisher
Who after forcing me to walk a lap around the park
Asked if I wanted to go get coffee
I replied . . .
Yes, after we stock up
At the 24-Hour liquor store

BOOZE

One thing you'll find
If you visit a 24-Hour liquor store
More often than not
Bulletproof glass will separate you
From the cashier
More often than not
Most of the brands are generic
Or worse
I asked for a bottle of Tanqueray
The best the cashier could offer
Was Phillips
I winced at the Publisher, who seemed
To be experiencing a morbid delight
In my lack of options
It was time to get serious
I screwed down my glance
Stopping on a bottle of Crown Royal
Remembering
What my son-in-law taught me
When most of your booze options are shit
Go with Crown Royal, if nothing else
At least you get a purple velvet bag
Out of the deal

DRIVE

Next up, espresso
I walked into a coffee shop
That looked like a coffee shop
That wanted to come across as . . . Progressive
Five or six employees bustled around the counter
Five or six employees looked up in unison
When I asked for an Americano on ice
Without the use of words or telepathy
I could tell by the softness in their smiles
That this coffee crew realized
I probably wasn't from Alabama
Or even from the South
I was a stranger in a strange land
That would more than certainly
Become the focal point
Of a three-minute conversation
Five seconds after I left

OPTIONS

The Publisher and I didn't need to be back
For my book signing until noon
I was tired and momentarily lacked motivation
This wasn't the Publisher's first time to Montgomery
Or the Fitzgerald Museum
I'm guessing maintaining a credible reputation
May have been important
Because I was told our decorum would improve
If we returned to our hosting venue
With several bottles of wine
To offset my jug of whiskey
I was given a choice to tag along
Browsing white wine aisles, and if time permitted
Maybe we could stop by a farmers' market
I asked to get dumped back at the park
Where I would be able to sit in silence
While finishing my espresso
Which may or may not have received
A bump of Crown Royal
The Publisher drove, I rifled through radio stations
Stopping at 107.1 the Vault – Album Rock
First, I heard a forgettable song, then I heard the next
SWEET HOME ALABAMA

HONESTLY

I didn't anticipate it happening
But it did
What were the chances
That we would hear SWEET HOME ALABAMA
In Alabama
After all the song was 48 years old
But then it occurred to me
Maybe it was just one of those things
At least down here
One of those things that never went away
Next it occurred to me
That even though I had heard this song 2,700 times
From here on out, every time I heard this song
Back at home, it would never be the same
Hand to God when you hear . . .
SWEET HOME ALABAMA
While driving through Alabama
It's a thing

ACCLIMATION

Even though I had a pretty good idea
That with just one look
Residents would find it easy to realize
I wasn't a local
It occurred to me that I should do my best
To assemble a wardrobe that paid tribute
To Southern sensibilities
Truth be told, I wasn't sure what that meant
I didn't own a velvet sports coat
Or a bow tie, anyway it was August
So, I just wore Ralph Lauren shorts
Nondescript T-shirts and a straw hat
A "Breaker" made by Stetson
When I put it on at home, and looked in the mirror
I had to smirk, I looked good
Even though I may have resembled a character
From a "Dukes of Hazzard" reboot
My hardest choice was footwear
No way in hell was I going to wear my Birkenstocks
That would just be asking for it
I thought about my bright pink Jordans
But I wore those at my last launch
At the Watergate Hotel
All that remained were two pairs of Doc Martens
One white, one black, I chose the latter

FITZGERALD PARK

After the Publisher dropped me at the park
I noticed a placard
That showed a fountain and a sun dial
Were given to the Fitzgeralds
Each of which got their own plaque
But I found it, well . . . funny's not the right word
So, I guess I'll just say I found it odd
That on Zelda's plaque it was stated
That these gifts were given to her
By her friends
But on Scott's plaque, gifts were listed
But there was no mention of friends
I felt sad for him
Next thing I noticed, there were two fountains
Zelda Fitzgerald fountains
One was being built, the other demolished
Neither one of them were at a point
Where they looked impressive
As I tried to imagine both versions in their splendor
People slowly crept across the grass
And joined me in the courtyard

45 MINUTES IN FITZGERALD PARK

Between the hours of 9 and 10
On a bench adjacent to mine
Sat a man who was not put together
A man in the grip of some battle
Big drops of rain began to fall
Rain drops by the tablespoon
The man refused to move
A woman with a terrier
Stopped as if she knew him
Offering dry escort
Underneath her umbrella
The man began to cry
What determines luck, who makes up the rules
Why is value attached to everything but me
The woman sat by his side
Put her arm around his shoulder
In silence the umbrella twirled
Until she offered explanation
Everything will be fine, she said
Just not today

A SORT OF HOMECOMING

I was told, via text, that the Executive Director
Of the museum was onsite, back at the Fitz
I don't know why, but it was very important to me
To gain the approval of the Executive Director
For a brief moment I considered this, and wondered
Why I cared as much as I did
But I did
And with that, I gained the realization
It didn't matter why, it was what it was
I cared, it was important to me
So, I mopped the sweat from my brow
Popped a breath mint
And made my way back to
919 Felder Avenue

INTRODUCTION

When I got back to the museum
I walked into the Gatsby Gallery
A room with a mantle, bookended by two mannequins
Clad in Brooks Brothers suits used in Leonardo DiCaprio's
"The Great Gatsby" film
Tick – Tock, I stood in silence
Tick – Tock, the Executive Director
Turned the corner and stared at me
With an ambivalent poker face
Tick – Tock, the silence pressed
I became nervous and blurted out . . .
So, are you more Fitzgerald or Gatsby
The Executive Director gave me a look
Indicating the answer was certain
Before replying . . .
Consider where you are
All of us here are devoted to Zelda
The obvious had eluded me
I wanted to crawl under a rock
I wanted to gain the approval
Of the Executive Director
I don't know why, but it was important to me

RIFFING

Within moments, the Executive Director and I
Were joined by the Publisher and
A Young Mother who did maintenance
On the museum, and
The Author from New York
Who wrote the book . . .
Stepping Out with Scott and Zelda:
Touring The Fitzgeralds' Montgomery
Somehow without me noticing
Our eclectic brood moved into a back room
Where itinerary was replaced with conversations
Concerning all things Fitzgerald
The Executive Director and the Author from New York
May have done as much scholarship on Zelda
As anyone in the world
Just to be in the conversation
Just to be in the conversation
Just to be in the conversation
Even though I was a little nervous
And very much out of my league, I hopped in
As if I were John Coltrane
Getting an introduction to Miles Davis

A SORT OF HOMECOMING

After the riff session grinded to a halt
There was an hour before my book signing started
Just as I was about to head upstairs, to my room
I was told I had a visitor
The guy's name was Billy
Billy lived in St. Paul
Our sons played baseball together, decades ago
Billy was on his way to Florida
To visit his dead father's second wife
He had seen a posting on social media
That I would be launching
The Dead Fitzgeralds
A book that he had actually bought in St. Paul
To read on his cross-country journey
At the time Billy saw the social media post
He was already in Montgomery
And my launch was still 36 hours away
But he stayed, he rented a motel room
And stuck around
God Damn, I was touched

THE LAUNCH

Even though the museum wasn't technically open
An exception was made for my cross-country friend
As everyone paid attention to last minute details
I marched Billy upstairs to the Zelda suite
My first instinct was to offer him the best
Of what I had, in this instance
That would have been Crown Royal
But it was only 12:50 p.m.
A touch early for many folks
So, I ended up fetching him a banana
And a Coke Zero, both of which he accepted
As he began peeling the peel
It was mentioned, just this morning
He had finished
The Dead Fitzgeralds
He gave the book a favorable critique
But truth be told, that didn't matter
What mattered was, I was happy
So, I offered Billy some Crown Royal
And he accepted

THE MOMENT

KNOCK – KNOCK, I answered the door
Across the threshold stood the Publisher
Flashing a look of indictment at Billy and me
For nursing cocktails in vintage tumblers
While the cap remained off the whiskey jug
I made the decision
Words weren't in my best interest
At the moment, so I retreated
In silence which was eventually broken
When the Publisher said quietly . . .
The table is set up in the Gatsby Gallery
Everyone's waiting for you, and by the way (pause)
The most highly regarded Fitzgerald Scholar on the planet
The guy you invited, 's here, waiting for you
Don't forget his gift, bring it downstairs
He's the good-looking guy, with a gray lion's mane
Then the Publisher performed a false exit
Just as the door was closed
Billy and I tilted our tumblers in the draining position
As the door popped open enough
For the Publisher to remind me
You said you were going to wear your baking whites
That's probably the play for this audience
So let's get a move on it

CHOP – CHOP GOES THE BAKER

As I headed toward the closet
To hop into my uniform
Billy thanked me for my hospitality
And wished me luck
I looked at the door, then back at the bottle
Billy smiled, so I poured us each
Two more fingers, as we drank
Neither of us spoke
After suiting up, I was busy
Making appropriate adjustments
To my apron and French baker's toque
When the whisky vanished
And I headed toward the door
Billy was kind enough to remind me . . .
Wasn't there supposed to be a gift

IN THE GATSBY GALLERY

The book table was set up
Covered with books and several Sharpies
I chose to bypass my immediate responsibility
To search out the Scholar
Within moments I found him stretched out
On the couch, smiling for whatever reason
I introduced myself and Billy as well
While noticing the Publisher wasn't lying
The Scholar had a thick gray mane
That had to invite discomfort
Especially during August in Bama
After salutations were issued
I mentioned even with a crew cut
I was sweating balls
The Scholar laughed, before explaining
When he first moved here
He couldn't move from one building to the next
Without getting drenched
But after a while, you simply get used to it
And if you don't, you just need to remember
To carry ice packs in your car

THE GIFT

I mentioned that at one point
I had sent him a note
Explaining I was going to send him a gift
The Scholar sent me the address
But for reasons out of my control
I wasn't able to secure the intended tribute
But as time passed, snow melted
And construction took place
So I was finally in a position
To liberate a brick paver
The brick weighed about twelve pounds
And was pulled from a spot
Outside the carriage house of James J. Hill
This was a spot Fitzgerald wrote so tenderly about
In his short story . . .
The Camel's Back

TRIBUTE

As the Scholar received the gift
His eyes sparkled, and as he held it
I marveled at how he carried it with such ease
I am a big man
A guy you would expect to have played on the offensive line
But the Scholar, he's built like a gymnast
Compact and muscular
The way he swung that brick inspired me
I explained to h m
How the TSA at MSP airport stopped me
And questioned the brick
Calling out that it could be classified as a weapon
To which I responded . . .
I'm heading to Bama
This is a gift of architecture
And who's kidding whc
My fists are bigger than bricks
This made the TSA supervisor laugh
And that made the Scholar laugh
Before encouraging me to consider
Stopping by the demolished Zelda fountair
To bring a brick back to St. Paul

MOMENTARY FAREWELLS

After books were signed
After closing salutations were dispensed
It was brought to my attention
That I had five hours to kill
Before heading to my next obligation
Billy said he'd meet me later that evening
At the nightclub
The Scholar and the Executive Director
Said the same
So I marched upstairs
Slipped out of my baker's whites
And into something less conspicuous

A SORT OF HOMECOMING

The Publisher said . . .
Get in the car, I did
We started towards downtown
I didn't ask where we were going
Figuring it wou d become apparent
The Publisher turned down the radio
And utilized a vocal tone
Reminiscent of a tour bus driver . . .
Up that hill is the 500 block
Of Pleasant Avenue
I believe Zelda's family, the Sayres,
Lived at 6 Pleasant Avenue
But later the city would restructure
The addresses in this neighborhood
Built on the remains of the Wilson Plantation
I've been to'd, this is either the oldest
Or one of the oldest residential
Areas in Montgomery

A SORT OF HOMECOMING

As we made our way up the hill
And turned onto the 500 block
This neighborhood which was once known
For its decadence had fallen on harder times
Most of the original Victorian
Queen Anne architecture had been replaced
By dilapidation and squalor
As we turned onto the 500 block
It wasn't hard to see
We were on top of a hill
In a place that once thrived
A place that looked over downtown
And the Alabama River
I tried to sense energy
From a better time
But the August heat was oppressive
And the relatively new freeway wall
Kind of crushed that vibe
Many of these fantastic structures
Were in disrepair
What was once great, now issued sadness

A SORT OF HOMECOMING

After turning into a dead end
The Publisher turned around
Indicating we had overshot
The lot where Zelda's childhood home
Once stood
Remember, the city had changed the addresses
So for once, numbers weren't going to be our friends
After the Publisher turned around
Cruising the rental car at trolling speed
The car once again stopped
While the Publisher said . . .
I do, I say I do declare
That vacant lot is where Zelda grew up
Think about it
Scott probably spent a lot of time
Right there, courting, waiting, hoping

A SORT OF HOMECOMING

To perceive what the Publisher announced
One would have to possess
More than a stellar imagination
From my vantage point
From the shotgun seat
All I could see was a chain-link fence
That masked a partial staircase
That was overgrown with weeds
And bramble
The Publisher went on to tell me
That Fitzgerald was once photographed
On these steps
I wasn't told by who or why
Because the topic immediately switched
To Scottie Fitzgerald Smith
And how she tried to save her mother's home
Hoping to turn it into some type of museum
But as I witnessed, the effort felt short
To gauge the temperature outside
I rolled down the window
Only to be overwhelmed by the heat
Jesus – Mary – Joseph
It was hot outside
And just like that, I became overwhelmed

PEACE AND JUSTICE

The Publisher engaged the ignition
Slipped the car into gear
The accelerator was engaged
Advancing with caution
We coasted down the hill
Originally, we rolled slowly
But as momentum picked up
Our speed increased
It became obvious I was uncomfortable
A reaction
That seemed to delight the Publisher
Halfway down the hill
The Publisher pressed the brake
Removed the keys from the ignition
Before ordering me to get out

PEACE AND JUSTICE

On the midst of the hill
Stood a structure
A monument
At first its appearance came off
As mathematic
Very geometrical
I'm only guessing here
But the campus that housed
The National Memorial for Peace and Justice appeared
to cover
A space the size of ten or twelve
Football fields
After the Publisher bought us tickets
We had to walk around structures
Made with complex angles
For the record, it was just about this point
I determined, the sun was scorching
Once we finally crossed the threshold
We were greeted by a sculpture
Of slaves chained together
I read their facial expressions as anguish
Truthfully, I became confused
The image disturbed me, I wanted to walk away

PEACE AND JUSTICE

But something told me
I was supposed to be disturbed
And if I wanted to honor the sculptor
I needed to stay put
To digest
So I did
And even though I had no idea
What to think
I just kept staring
Until departure seemed natural
Across six acres
There were 800 six-foot monuments
I think they were made from granite
Or something that resembled granite
Each one of these was about the size
Of a modern refrigerator
And on these 800 six-foot monuments
Were carved the names of 4,400 victims
Who were terrorized and lynched

PEACE AND JUSTICE

As the Publisher and I advanced
We didn't speak
It wasn't the type of place
Where you'd say things
That didn't merit being said
As the Publisher and I advanced
I remembered a book I'd read
The Lynchings in Duluth
By Michael Fedo
The book was well written
Three African American men
Accused of a crime
They probably didn't commit
The town folks went berserk
And thousands of them
Five thousand if I remember correctly
Filled the street
In front of the jail
Thousands . . .
The few jailors stood firm
Atticus Finch-like
But the mob ruled
And blood was spilled

PEACE AND JUSTICE

As the Publisher and I advanced
Our path crossed an attendant
A young man seated at a table
I told him about the book I read
About the three men from Duluth
Who fell victim to the mob's fury
I told him that all the monuments
I had seen were from Southern states
I asked if there were any from Minnesota
The young man nodded
Asked me to follow
Marching the Publisher and I
Outside the primary structure
To a group of monuments outside
Along the perimeter
The young man pointed
Speaking softly, he said . . .
We only have one monument
From Minnesota
That's it right there

PEACE AND JUSTICE

The Minnesota monument
Was laying down, in coffin position
It had Minnesota
Duluth and St. Louis County
Listed on the front of the tomb
On the top were the names
Of the fallen men

ELMER JACKSON
06 15 1920

ISAAC MCGHIE
06 15 1920

ELIAS CLAYTON
06 15 1920

PEACE AND JUSTICE

I don't know if it was wrong or right
But I felt grateful these three men were honored
On this sacred space
I felt honored
To pay respect, from myself
And on behalf cf Michael Fedo

PEACE AND JUSTICE

After our tour was complete, we stepped outside
Of the installation's perimeter
Where I overheard
A woman in a blue dress
Tell a woman in a white dress
That one of the reasons
The city gifted the land to the monument
Was because that part of the city was run down
The property held no value
However, once the monument was completed
People came to see it
People from near and far
The woman in the white dress announced . . .
That the experience was haunting
But she was very much moved by it
To which the woman in the blue dress replied . . .
You and many others, recently somebody told me
Just before the pandemic hit
This monument was bringing more than one million dollars
Into Montgomery, annually

DEXTER AVENUE

Next stop, the famous Court Square fountain
The fountain I had always been led to believe
Zelda jumped into, naked
It would be later in the day
When I would learn from the Executive Director
Zelda wasn't actually naked
She was wearing a flesh-colored
Annette Kellerman swimsuit
The fountain was gorgeous
Cast-iron, and impressive
I've never claimed to be
An authority on fountains
But gosh, this fountain was unique
As far as fountains go
On top, a cupbearer to the Greek gods
And the goddess of eternal youth
There's also a bunch of kids
But if you ask me, kids always look creepy
On fountains or in statue form
One last detail that impressed me
The designer didn't take the easy way out
By casting traditional eagles
Instead, a sedge of cranes was used
Grooming themselves with delight

DOWN THE STREET

Just about a stone's throw away
From the Court Square fountain
Is a statue of Rosa Parks
Standing on the street corner
Where she caught the bus
On the day she decided to defy insanity
As I stared at the statue, I thought about stuff
Things that made me think about things
Things that made me uncertain
I began to feel naïve
I wondered if an old Yankee
With limited time in the deep South
Could even begin to wrap their mind
Around the complexities that exist there
Then I started to feel naïve
Until for no reason in particular
It struck me, how curious it was
How fortunate I was
That I was in a space
Shared by Zelda and Rosa
That had to be a thing
Right?

JACKPOT

The mistreatment of people swam through my mind
One thought crashed into another
I thought about the Holocaust Museum in DC
The peril of the Jews, Poles, Czechs and others
I thought about the Mexicans in St. Paul
How the Capital City makes the claim
They are a sanctuary city
But when ICE trolls through the neighborhood
White people turn their backs
While withholding resources
Then my mind went back to the airport
To the moment when I found out
Salman Rushdie had been stabbed
I felt sad, I felt useless
Until these feelings were replaced
By a sense of foolishness
Because I had never read Salman Rushdie
That thought returned me to sad

JACKPOT

I decided I wanted to buy a book
A Salman Rushdie book
I wanted to buy the book
That encouraged the fatwa
I asked the Publisher for the title
And because the Publisher
Is a publisher, it was made clear
I needed to buy
The Satanic Verses
I needed to buy the book
That encouraged the fatwa
So, I asked the Publisher for help
And . . .Zoom
Within moments we arrived at the most
Beautiful dumpy bookstore I had been to
In a long time . . .
BOOKS – A – MILLION
Behind a counter was a woman
Who I confided in
After finding me a copy
Of my request
She mentioned it was the second one
She had sold that day

TWO HOURS UNTIL SHOWTIME

When I looked at my phone
I realized if we went back to our lodging
I would have just about 100 minutes
To unwind and mentally prepare
For my evening at the Hilltop nightclub
Where I would be presenting
A Zelda trivia contest and reading fortunes
With my tarot deck
I didn't have any knowedge
Concerning the venue
Stage size
Lighting
Sound system
I didn't have a clue
Several times when I asked the Publisher
The only response I was given was advice
I was told to relax, to ride the wave
When I looked at my phone again
I realized I had 94 minutes
To unwind and mentally prepare

FITZGERALD PARK

Alone
I sat
Alone
I thumbed through pages of
The Satanic Verses
I wanted to read
But realized it was useless
Alone
I sat
Motionless
I wanted to read
But realized it was pointless
I asked my phone
To relay Salman's current condition
A story popped up
An interview with the mother
Of the man who attacked Salman
The attacker's mom said . . .
She was surprised
She didn't see this coming
But her son made a choice
And acted out on it
There should be accountability
She would speak to him no more

FITZGERALD PARK

Then I thought about the monument
I thought how glad I was
That the author of
The Duluth Lynchings
Had helped me erase an entry-level
Amount of ignorance
Not that it mattered, but I wondered
Was the author, was Michael Fedo
Even alive
I asked my phone
It said he was
So, it did matter
Enough at least for me
To search out his contact information
I found it
I wondered what I should say
I wasn't sure what would matter
So I told the truth

FITZGERALD PARK

Mr. Fedo
I live in St. Paul
I am a Master Bread Baker
Who has been baking 42 years
I traveled to Montgomery Alabama
During the trip, I stopped at
The National Memorial for Peace and Justice
It's a HUGE installation
Showing African Americans
Who have been murdered
I read your book
I love your book
It's so well written
I asked an employee
If the three men from Duluth
Were represented, they were
I was proud to honor them
On your behalf
In your debt . . .
The Baker

FITZGERALD PARK

I sat
Alone
On a bench
Looking at the Zelda fountains
Which were circular brick patterns
About shin high
Both projects appeared stalled
I wondered why
Would you demolish one fountain
80% of the way, and stop
And then start a second fountain
20% of the way, and stop
Leaving them next to each other
In adjacent position
I would have blown up the first
Cleaned up evidence of its existence
Then placed the new fountain
Over the old site
But I'm not a fountain expert
Maybe there were plumbing issues
Or some such thing
Either way, the visual left me confused
And disappointed

FITZGERALD PARK

I considered how much this neighborhood
Cloverdale
Looked like my neighborhood
Crocus Hill
Mansions
Cobblestones
Lush green this
Lush green that
People walking the streets
As if they have nowhere to be
So they just walk
And wonder about things
Most of which might bore me
I looked across the street
And saw Helen Keller's sister's house
Realizing
They had to have come here
Countless times
To this very spot
Possibly in the presence of Zelda
My allurement was sidetracked
When a bug flew into my eye
The collision made me forget
What I was wondering

FITZGERALD PARK

I thought about the evening's show
Until I decided I should be focusing
On the park
Because I like parks
I loved this park
Not one to wade into pools of regret
I caught myself
Momentarily feeling sorry for myself
Once I considered
For close to a century
People have come to this park
And enjoyed a beautiful fountain
Then it occurred to me
I had no idea what these fountains looked like
But in my mind's eye
I was pretty sure they were, or would be pretty
Then it occurred to me
For maybe another century
People will get to enjoy the next fountain
And for no other reason than
The gods tend to be cruel
I will know of their majestic presence
But may never have the opportunity
To see either, n their completion

FITZGERALD PARK

I sat
Alone
At the point where thinking
Begins to segue with drifting
The lull lifted
The moment I heard
A helicopter flying overhead
Then, for the first time
Of all the times
I've heard a helicopter fly overhead
It occurred to me
Every time a helicopter passes by
Something really good
Or really bad
Is happening
I wondered which it was
In this instance

FITZGERALD PARK

I have no idea
Why I think, some of the things
I think, or where their influences
Come from
But there I was sweating
On a park bench
Rifling through the pages of
The Satanic Verses
A book which I hadn't read
But there I was
Staring – Staring – Staring
At Salman Rushdie
Or more correctly, his author picture
And then it struck me
His spirit was strong, his spirit was forgiving
My hunch was, he was
Saddened for the 'ost soul who upended his life
And then it struck me
I had no right to impose my wonder
On Salman Rushdie's circumstance
But I couldn't help it

FITZGERALD PARK

I sat
Alone
My body was beginning to acclimate
To the Alabama heat
To the realization
That I had been in this city
But had seen almost nobody
The streets were quiet
Quiet until, a Dodge minivan drove by
Windows rolled down
Music blaring
The song of the moment was
FEELS SO GOOD
By Chuck Mangione
Possibly the only person
To top the pop charts
Playing a flugelhorn

FITZGERALD PARK

I used to love that song
It was beyond popular
When I was 14
I remember how much I enjoyed it
While peddling my bicycle to work
But as much as I loved this song
I wasn't allowed to admit it
Because I was 14
And nothing was more important
At this age than being cool
By my neighborhood's standards
There was nothing cool
About a man who wore a silly hat
And played the flugelhorn

FITZGERALD PARK

Back on my phone
I thumbed across a story
Anne Frank had been banned
And pulled off the bookshelves
Of schools in a particular part
Of Texas
God Dammit
This made me angry
On many levels
I always pull for Texas
I find it meets more of my sensibilities
Than any state in the nation
But to pull Anne Frank is whack
The story said, there are several versions
Of Anne Frank
But her father edited it
And pulled much of its content
Apparently young Anne made a statement
Where she mentioned being attracted to women
And that was enough
Texas pulled it off the shelf
And the Nazis win one more battle

FITZGERALD PARK

I wondered
If a person was capable of not thinking
Because even when you don't want to
You inadvertertly do
When you go to sleep
Dreams fill your mind
I wondered
Were dreams an overflow
Of thought
I stared at the fountains
Both of which were uncompleted
And I made a pact
To return
After the second one was complete
Even if it meant forfeiting
A travel experience to places unseen
Like Myrtle Beach, Hollywood or Montana

FITZGERALD PARK

I looked at my phone
The time announced
It was almost time for me
To get cleaned up
And head to the show
My stint in Bama
Was halfway complete
There was no way
I was going to get to see
Everything that should be seen
Everything I wanted to see
It would have been interesting
To trace the footsteps
Of Hank Williams
Of Martin Luther King
Of Jefferson Davis
But these things would have to wait
For if and when I returned

HILLTOP NIGHTCLUB

This was the gig
My Montgomery contacts promoted
A Zelda trivia contest, as well as tarot readings
I would look into the futures of
Partygoers that would make Warhol swoon
It may have been one of the most eclectic
Groups I have been a part of
Straight – Queer – Black – White
Scholars – Dropouts – Beauticians – Musicians
Outside there were food trucks, inside there was booze
Outside it was sweltering, inside was even hotter
Less than an hour after kickoff
A pack of women entered my space, laughing
Discussing how some tart next door
Kept lifting her skirt, flashing her womanhood
In the direction of some guitar guy
Named Bobby Apple
It was hot, I was thirsty
I ordered a Tanqueray & Tonic
Only to be told . . .
This is Bama, son, we do it different down here
Then orders were issued, orders to no one in particular
To fetch me a shot of Gunpowder

HILLTOP NIGHTCLUB

I was skeptical
I was annoyed
But I was also
A stranger in a strange land
So I adhered to traveler's law
"When In Rome"
Thus, I raised, tilted and poured
The tumbler's contents
Praise the Lord
I felt thunder
Move through my body
As if I was filled by the Holy Spirit
Not to be sacrilegious
But finding a new gin
Better than Tanqueray
Is just about as hard
As finding a new deity
That can go toe to toe
With Jesus

HILLTOP NIGHTCLUB

Everybody from the earlier event arrived
The Publisher
The Executive Director
The Fitzgerald Scholar
Even the Young Mother
Most of these folks mingled
Amongst the vampires
Once the audience was intact
I did the Zelda Trivia set
Prizes were given away
People were drunk, people were sweaty
Just as I prepared to set up the tarot table
My home slice Billy came barreling in
Through the door, setting his cocktail
On my table, while he talked
To the Executive Director
Once his attention was diverted
I picked up his tumbler, took a glug
Before wincing, and asking . . .
Are you serious Billy, an Old Fashioned
To which he responded . . .
All night long

HILLTOP NIGHTCLUB

Somewhere from the crowd
Somebody said something
About the filmmaker Fellini
The second I heard this, I shrugged
With the realization
This was going to be a weird night
But things got even weirder
When Billy kept the topic alive
By issuing his dilettante narrative

HILLTOP NIGHTCLUB

Billy said . . .
Fellini loved Hitchcock
He loved his film
"The Birds"
But he was disappointed how it ended
Remember how Tippi and her companions
Slinked out of the house
And waded through a pile of crows
Before hopping into a car and driving away
That wasn't a horrible ending
But it was random at best
I heard, originally Hitch wanted
To end the film with a shot
Of the Golden Gate Bridge
Covered entirely by crows
In fact, Hitchcock was quoted
And I'm paraphrasing here
But he said something like . . .
Would have been a perfect ending
An Apocalyptic poem

HILLTOP NIGHTCLUB

God – D
I loved that movie
I've seen it a dozen times
Sometimes I still get nightmares
Retracing the scene where Mr. Howell
From "Gilligan's Island"
Got his eyes plucked out by seagulls
While he tried so desperately to
Gain sanctuary in the phone booth
Occupied by Tippi Hedren
At this point, a voice from the crowd declared . . .
I would love to occupy Tippi
While someone else asked
If she was even alive
I smiled, I liked Bama
And its cast of kooks
God – D
I don't make a habit out of correcting filmmakers
But Hitchcock fumbled on the goal line
That film should have closed
With crows covering the Golden Gate Bridge

HILLTOP NIGHTCLUB

Intrigued as I was with the Hitchcock conversation
It was time to shift gears
Time to get another Gunpowder
But this time add some tonic
After taking a deep breath
I set up my clipboard, shuffled my tarot deck
And was just about ready to open for business
When some woman I had never met asked me . . .
Is Melanie Griffith
Tippi Hedren's daughter
I didn't know. I had never heard that
I was just about to ask Billy
But the Publisher beat me to the punch
And verified the claim to be true
SHUFFLE – SHUFFLE – SHUFFLE
Step right up, fortunes told, don't be afraid
Step right up, relax, and see what's in store for you
Who wants to go first

HILLTOP NIGHTCLUB

At one point prior to the show starting
The woman in charge of the sound system
Asked me what kind of music I wanted
To set the mood for fortune telling
To tell the truth, I hadn't thought about this
So, keeping in the spirit of
"When In Rome"
I said play whatever you think
Will work best with this crowd
So, according to the sound system gal
People were about to meet their destiny
While being accompanied with a soundtrack
Provided by . . .
The Wu-Tang Clan

HILLTOP NIGHTCLUB

Afros and mullets
Waiting their turn
Standing in line
Waiting their turn
To look into the future
Their only requirement
To think of a question
That they can say out loud
Or keep to themselves
Most of the people
Keep their question to themselves
As if I didn't already know
What was on their mind

HILLTOP NIGHTCLUB

A couple with a wardrobe
That announced them to be
Better off than most of the people at the event
Approached the table, he went first
Keeping his question to himself
After the cards were revealed
And their meaning was discussed
He asked his partner
If she wanted to know his question
She didn't answer, he told her anyway
Next, she sat across from me
Keeping her question to herself
After the cards were revealed
And the meaning was discussed
He wanted to know her question
She wouldn't tell him
Nothing else was said
The couple left without speaking

HILLTOP NIGHTCLUB

Between sets
Guitar guy Bobby Apple swung by
For a reading
I asked him if he had his question
He did
I spread out three cards
But before I flipped them over
I told Bobby Apple
I was having a premonition
He looked startled
I tried not to grin
Before telling him
I had it on good authority
That sometime tonight
A woman would hike up her skirt
And flash her womanhood
In your direction
Bobby Apple didn't stick around
To watch me flip his cards
He just smiled, and blushed
While exiting out back

HILLTOP NIGHTCLUB

Afros and mullets
Standing in line
Waiting their turn
From the huddle
I heard somebody use the phrase
"The heart of Dixie"
I asked what that meant
And if "Dixie"
Was a socially acceptable phrase
One of the mullets flashed an odd expression
Before explaining
It's Alabama's most popular nickname
I sat silent
Scanned the crowd
Searching for a single objection

HILLTOP NIGHTCLUB

As the next querent took their seat
I spoke into the crowd
Asking nobody in particular . . .
What about the Dixie Chicks
They dropped the Dixie part
And now they're simply the Chicks
The first response came from a mullet
Who claimed, whoever they are
Chicks or Dixie Chicks
They should be embarrassed
By their cover of Fleetwood Mac's
LANDSLIDE
I took exception to this, stating
The Chicks crushed it
Their version was much better
Then somebody from the back
Of the huddle, made a comment
About how "hot" the pregnant chick
From the Dixie Chicks, or Chicks
Was in that video
The comment made me uncomfortable
So I returned my attention
Back to the cards

HILLTOP NIGHTCLUB

I had been reading fortunes for five hours
Maybe six
I never made it to the food truck
Or got to see Bobby Apple perform
Several times I thought I was finished
So much for false alarms
These guys kept me working so hard
I didn't even have a chance to pee
The last woman to approach me explained . . .
I'm pretty sure what my cards will say
When you're a Black girl
Who gets adopted by a white family
Living in Salt Lake City
The deck is already stacked against you
The comment had sharp corners
There were several ways to respond
I chose smiling, and assuring her . . .
Yep, I'm pretty certain you're doomed
How about we just forget these cards
And have ourselves a drink
She smiled while giving me an innocent hug
And that was a wrap

MORE COCKTAILS

When the Publisher and I
Returned to our lodging
I mentioned I was considering
Grabbing my jug of whiskey
And coming back outside
To sip cocktails, in the front yard
Underneath the magnolia tree
Up the stairs
In my room
Snatch the bottle
Down the stairs
Cross the yard
Lawn chairs and heat
A perfect environment
To relax and recline

MORE COCKTAILS

Everything was perfect
I was drunk, with the knowledge
That I was about to add layers
Of drunkenness onto that
The cicadas were humming
If that's what in fact, they do
I waited for a moment
For the Publisher to join me
Everything was perfect
So I felt it best to proceed
By pouring a drink
And looking across the lawn
At shadows of a terrain
That couldn't be less familiar
GLUG – GLUG I wondered
GLUG – GLUG I considered
Just how stretched I'd feel
Five hours later
When my alarm went off
It didn't seem to matter
Everything was perfect

MORE COCKTAILS

Where was the Publisher
Oh well, what did it matter
You do you
I'll do me
GLUG – GLUG
Glance at my phone
Pictures – Pictures
Pictures and social media
Then, Blammo
What was I thinking
I began surfing emails
Only to find, I got a response
From the author of
The Lynchings in Duluth
Michael Fedo

MORE COCKTAILS

He said . . .
Thank you for your letter
Regarding my Duluth book
It's been a long journey
This book first appeared in 1979
To considerable under-appreciation
I received blowback from
(A publisher I won't mention)
Operating under the principal
If you can't say anything nice about Minnesota
Don't say anything at all
(Then he names a newspaper I won't mention)
Chided me for resurrecting the story
And rubbing our noses in it, all over again
The original publisher, a small California firm
Went bankrupt a month later
Though I was awarded $260 by the court
Which I used to buy tires for the 1968
Dodge I was driving at the time
Then Michael began talking about
A children's publisher in Paris
The font began to blur, forcing me
To shut off my phone

MORE COCKTAILS

As I sat
As I swayed with the moment
The Publisher crossed the lawn
Sat in a chair next to mine
Holding a bottle of wine
For about a million years
We didn't talk
We just absorbed the heat
God – D those cicadas are a thing
They seem to possess hypnotic qualities
Everything was perfect
At one point, the silence was broken
By a drunken voice, the Publisher
Slurred pleasantly about Zelda
And the letters she wrote in 1930
While she was held hostage
In a sanitarium in Switzerland
According to the Publisher
Zelda gave beautiful descriptions
Of velvet nights
Then she informed me, I could find those letters
On a Paris Review website
Everything was perfect
Until the bottles ran dry

MORE COCKTAILS

If you are accomplished in cocktailing
You may have experienced
Sometimes on the days God doesn't hate you
You can drink and drink
Drink yourself to drunk
Drink yourself to disorientation
Drink yourself to blackout
And for reasons that may or may not
Escape explanation
Biology and caloric intake
Can be enough to drag a soul
Though a tube of drunkenness
And out the other side, unscathed
This was one of those rare moments
A moment appropriate to issue gratitude
But my voice was parched
And the sky was velvet
The Publisher had disappeared
And the lawn was weary of my presence

ZELDA FITZGERALD'S BED

After a Coke Zero
Washing my face
And brushing my teeth
I retired to Zelda Fitzgerald's bedroom
I think I mentioned it earlier
But if you forgot
I would be remiss if I didn't remind you
It has been reported Zelda and Scott
Kept separate sleeping chambers
Something about this
Something I probably don't need to explain
Seemed to make me happy
The previous night
Travel lag had made me world weary
And I passed out immediately
An opportunity wasted
A mistake I desperately didn't want
To replicate

ZELDA FITZGERALD'S BED

In no particular order
High ceilings
Period appropriate artwork
Period appropriate furniture
No television
No radio
Heavy velvet drapes
Blackout curtain
And . . .
A lifetime supply of pillows
That covered a bed
Large enough to make one consider
Things of notable size
Things like an aircraft carrier
Or Cincinnati

ZELDA FITZGERALD'S BED

Amidst the silence
Amidst the calm
I began to notice certain energy
Occupied this space
I felt the energy was familiar
But I couldn't put my finger on it
What was it
I tried to move on
But my inability to clarify this burden
Annoyed me
Pebble in a shoe annoyed me
Amidst the silence
Amidst the calm
I reached out for a rational explanation
But came up empty, fell forward
Stretched out, on top of the covers
Lying face down, across the bed
The room contained no bird pictures
That kind of surprised me
It really seemed like a room
That should have bird pictures

ZELDA FITZGERALD'S BED

I did as the Publisher suggested
And found an article online
An excerpt from the Paris Review
That ran a series of letters
Written by Zelda, in the autumn of 1930
While she was locked up at a clinic
In Nyon, Switzerland (13 months)
The letters were all written to Scott
I read the letters several times
The content confused me
They were well written
Yet the topics at times seemed random
For instance
Zelda starts off one letter saying . . .
Dear,
Good night
Then she typed the word "Dear"
62 more times, and that was it

ZELDA FITZGERALD'S BED

It scared me, think about it
Think about where I was
Think about my altered state
My first thought was that scene in the movie
"The Shining"
Where Shelley Duvall finds
Jack Nicholson's manuscript
Repeating line after line . . .
All work and no play makes Jack a dull boy
Sometimes, as in this instance
Random can become more creepy than creepy

ZELDA FITZGERALD'S BED

Another one from the autumn of 1930
Zelda writes . . .
You do not look like a person
Plowing a storm
But like a person very surprised
At their means of locomotion

ZELDA FITZGERALD'S BED

I had no idea what that meant
I thought it was clever
And the poet in me wanted to
Secretly stash that phrase
To claim some version of it
As my own later
But the more I read these letters
It occurred to me that Zelda
Was auditioning for her husband's love
Or at least his attention
I remained motionless
The room's energy remained off-balance
I remained quiet, thinking . . .
This is the room she slept in
Once she was released from Switzerland
Apparently, I hadn't employed
My blackout curtain properly
I could see the first tones of light, entering
It was at that moment
The answer came to me, the energy in this room
Revolved around forgiveness
A room where forgiveness would be offered
If not received

ZELDA FITZGERALD'S BED

In real time, it's hard to notice
Silence without exception
Leads up to
The crescendo of a moment
I sat in silence, scrolling
Continuing the Switzerland letters
In which Zelda said . . .
Hasn't it been a lovely day
I woke up this morning
And the sun was lying
Like a birthday parcel
On my table
So I opened it up
And so many happy things
Went fluttering into the air

ZELDA FITZGERALD'S BED

In real time, it's hard to notice
Silence without exception
Leads up to
The crescendo of a moment
I sat in silence, considering this trip
I had assumed a message of some sort
Would be given to me
In Zelda's bedroom
But for reasons unknown
I just assumed connection
Would be made at night
Under the cover of darkness
My perception couldn't have been
More off track, I sat
I sat in silence
Amidst light in abundance
Amidst joy in abundance
I sat in silence
Until I experienced
The crescendo of the moment

ZELDA FITZGERALD'S BED

A thought occurred to me
The answer occurred to me
I began to feel their presence
As I crawled off the bed
Toward the window
And slowly peeled back
The blackout curtains
What I saw made me quake
I never knew, but now I did
I imagine they are everywhere
But I'd never seen them
Until I entered Montgomery
Where the Alabama sky
Was filled with angels

INTERMISSION

FITZGERALD PARK

For those of you
Who travel more than most
Yet less than mary
I'm guessing you'll understand
The dialogue that takes place
Between your mind and subconscious
When you spend time in a new city
Conversations take place
Inside your skull
That you're not fully aware of
Conversations where you
Discuss with you
If returning to this city
Is a viable option
As I sat on the park bench
I overheard me, talking to me
Deep inside my skull
I heard a quiet voice say . . .
I will return

FITZGERALD PARK

The sun was yawning
The magnolia stretched
There was so much more
About Montgomery
About Zelda
That I wanted to discover
But I sat alone
Thinking about things
Overthinking things
Things concerning the future
Things buried in the past
The sun was yawning
The magnolia stretched
As it occurred to me
I felt dizzy
And might have been
Two levels past parched

FITZGERALD PARK

Sometimes you think about things
Because they are connected to reason
Or situations
Other times you think about things
Because it's impossible
To shut down your mind
Mental debris whirls
Causing random moments
To stand at attention
And be pondered
Such was the case
When I began thinking
About Statue Man

FITZGERALD PARK

It all started with my Tarot Teacher
Because she's inner circle
I gave her an advanced copy of
The Dead Fitzgeralds
To which she responded . . .
I'm so glad you mentioned
The Nathan Hale statue
And the F. Scott one, as well
Or did you mention the F. Scott one
Anyway
A friend of mine
A guy we call Bilbo
He's the guy who fixed the Hale statue
He also cast Fitzgerald
As a matter of fact
I was with him at the unveiling
That was years ago
I think Paul Wellstone
And Garrison Keillor were there

FITZGERALD PARK

I don't know why this intrigued me
But it did, a lot
I wanted to meet Statue Man
And check out his gallery
Tarot Teacher told me
He lived an hour away
On a farm, so many acres
So many acres, so many acres
You had to wear shit kickers
Because in addition to sculpting
Statue Man had cows
40 of them
I don't know why this intrigued me
But it did, a lot

FITZGERALD PARK

At the farm, at the studio
Everything was just as you might expect
Bales of hay, dogs, cracker boxes
Posters from baseball seasons, decades past
Statue Man was gracious
I mentioned I only counted 24 cows
Not 40, he said the actual number was 28
I remained silent, until he continued . . .
Drought, it's bad, I had to sell a dozen head
Everybody around here was forced to sell early

FITZGERALD PARK

I never asked why they called him Bilbo
In fact, if we were in Middle Earth
With those broad shoulders and thick beard
Statue Man might have passed for a dwarf
He looked a bit like Gimli
With those hands the size of catcher mitts
And eyes brighter than innocence
He looked like someone you could trust
After wading through trinkets and tools
Statue Man pointed to one of the few empty
Spaces within the barn
He explained, this is where he worked on
His most recent commission
A statue of a Red Wing boot
That was shipped to Kuwait

FITZGERALD PARK

When the topic turned to the Nathan Hale statue
Statue Man made references
To techniques used to save
Yet another monument, from the scrap heap
When I asked for a bit of information
Concerning the Fitzgerald statue
Something most people didn't know
Statue Man grinned big, before explaining . . .
That's easy
Remember, I didn't design that sculpture
I just cast it
But the guy who designed it
It turned out he was displeased with Scott's head
It bothered him so much
He chopped it clean off the body
A second head had to be made and attached

FITZGERALD PARK

Church bells began to ring
As people slowly entered my space
With each passing moment
Distractions would multiply
So I decided to p ace
Tarot Teacher and Statue Man
Somewhere comfortable
In my mental warehouse
Not long after, I spied the Publisher
Crossing the park
I assumed I would note
A staggering gate
Or bloodshot eyes
That wasn't the case, not even close
The Publisher was chipper
So much so, I was instructed
To gather my things
We were heading to the graveyard

OAKWOOD CEMETERY

I spent the morning looking
At Confederate soldiers' grave markers
Cicadas screeched
Trains whistled, down in the valley
Trees had moss
Spanish moss draping
Everything was wet
Ideal conditions for healthy skin
But murder on the hair
A guy followed me
Wearing a T-shirt stating
We Shall Prevail
What did that mean, why was he tailing me
Upon further investigation, I deduced
He was KGB, or an insurance salesman
Haze and dew
Dew on my boots
Bugs bigger than dragons
I was out of my element
Which isn't a bad thing
On a Sunday morning

OAKWOOD CEMETERY

The Publisher mentioned
Somewhere close was a vault
Where Zelda liked to flirt
With gentlemen callers
The Publisher mentioned
At this vault Zelda
Wrote something provocative enough
To capture Scott's attention
A romantic caption
That Scott would "borrow"
And use toward the end
Of his debut novel
The Publisher mentioned
The provocative quote
Was so provocative
That somebody, somewhere
From some Fitzgerald organization
Put the quote on the front
Of a decorative postcard

OAKWOOD CEMETERY

The Publisher thought they knew
The location of the vault
Minutes passed, into . . .
Quarter hours
Half hours
The sun showed no mercy
I was as parched as that guy
You see in every desert movie
Who succumbs to dehydration
Knowing I was close to death
I displayed whining expressions
That went unnoticed
The Publisher diddled and dallied
At every plot possessing a headstone
The size of this final resting place
Would not receive proper recognition
If you simply listed square acreage
To pay proper respect
One needs to take into account
How the size seems increased
Due to rolling hills covered with trees
That seemed almost as tall as Sequoias

OAKWOOD CEMETERY

As I trudged on, I found myself alone
At the foot of a hill where countless
Confederate soldiers had been buried
As I climbed the hill
And walked between the grave markers
It made me sad that each cross
Stood crooked, tilted at a 90-degree angle
As I trudged on, I found myself sad
Realizing these guys have to spend eternity
Lying in an unnatural position
Then I began to wonder if tranquility
Was something that could only be enjoyed
On flat terrain, void of elevation
At the top of the hill
I considered my Yankee status
And truth be told
I don't have sympathy for the ideals
The Confederates fought to preserve
But right is right, right?
I would never consider burying
My worst enemy in or on a lopsided plot
So who, how and why
Why were these brave men placed
In a place of torment, by their own kin

OAKWOOD CEMETERY

Fast forward to eternity's end
Then add another 90 minutes
That's when I rediscovered the Publisher
Taking selfies in what turned out to be
A collection of graveyard obelisk photos
That had to number in the hundreds
I don't think it was even 10 a.m.
And I was already in need of a second shower
I asked about the vault
When the Publisher didn't respond
I chalked up silence, to surrender
Silence issued procedure
Get in the car
Get out of Dodge
And dump my ass off
At either an oasis
Or the Fitzgerald Museum

REBOOT

Meanwhile . . . back at the museum
Before the first Coke Zero was drained
The second was tilted
GULP – GULP
Refreshment overdue
As I considered a third
The Executive Director entered
Asked what was new
I mentioned the morning's debacle
This brought joy to our host
Who ordered remedy
Who ordered me to fetch
The Publisher so we could head back
To where our purpose had faltered previously

OAKWOOD CEMETERY

The Executive Director directed our entry
To a different entrance
An entrance close to the graves
Occupied by Hank Williams
And other members of his family
Out of the approximate billion gravesites
At Oakwood Cemetery, the Williams family site
Had the only plots surrounded by Astroturf
Typically, dead cowboys are a topic
That would flip my switch
But on this day, not so much
In my mind, this day, this moment
Was all about Zelda
The Executive Director
Ordered us back into the car
The Executive Director didn't seem in a hurry
CHUG –CHUG, we passed through silence
Maintaining rowboat speed

OAKWOOD CEMETERY

Everybody out
Announced the Executive Director
While pointing to a luscious view
Isn't it beautiful
Announced the Executive Director
Those plots were recently purchased
By my family
One day I will be buried there

OAKWOOD CEMETERY

Everybody out
Announced the Executive Director
As we rolled to a stop
On top of a steep slope
Facing a deeply wooded area
Without certainty
Of where we were going
Or what we were doing
Each of us employed cautious footwork
As we descended halfway down
And just like that, there it was
The vault that was so special to Zelda
To be truthful, the vault was disorienting
It was rustically beautiful
While maintaining horrific qualities
At first glance, I couldn't be certain
Of this structure's purpose
I assumed it contained dead people
It was beautiful, it was horrific

OAKWOOD CEMETERY

It was beautiful, it was horrific
Like a Francis Bacon painting
Like a Black Sabbath album cover
I think I was mesmerized
Transfixed
As I stood tilted on the hill
The Executive Director
Handed me a decorative postcard
With the quote F Scott "borrowed"
From Zelda

OAKWOOD CEMETERY

"I've spent today in the graveyard
It really isn't a cemetery, you know
Trying to unlock a rusty iron vault
Built in the side of a hill
It's all washed and covered with weepy
Watery blue flowers
That might have grown from dead eyes
Sticky to touch with a sickening odor
The boys wanted to go, to test my nerve
Tonight, I wanted to feel (William Wreford) 1864
Why should graves make people feel in vain
I've heard so much, and Gray is so convincing
But somehow, I can't find anything hopeless
In having lived
All the broken columns and clasped hands
And doves and angels mean romances"
That's only the first half of the postcard
But the writing was so beautiful
Before my eyes I watched the vault
Transform into something just short
Of a holy relic

OAKWOOD CEMETERY

I continued reading the second portion
"And in a hundred years I think I shall like
Having young people speculate
On whether my eyes were brown or blue
Of course, they are neither
I hope my grave has an air
Of many, many years on it, isn't it funny how
A row of Confederate soldiers
Will make you think of dead loves
When they're exactly like the others
Even to the yellowish moss
Old death is so beautiful
So very beautiful
We will die together
I know
Sweetheart"

OAKWOOD CEMETERY

With that, I went limp, numb
Energy surged through me
As if I was standing over a portal
My mind began to flood
With gratitude, I felt honored
To stand in the midst of Zelda's youth
A period which might have been
The happiest point of her life

OAKWOOD CEMETERY

The Executive Director didn't say a word
The Publisher remained silent
We just stood, motionless
The heat increased
While bugs and birds fell silent
The usual me, would have taken this moment
To consider a third shower
But hygiene had fallen to the wayside
All I could think about was
How important it was to Zelda
To be buried someplace with panache
In a place, on a space where people would gather
Wonder, enjoy and consider her essence
All I could think about was
How she wanted her final resting place
To be shrouded with mojo and patina
Then I stopped to consider
Her gravesite in Rockville Maryland
And with that, every bit of luster I had accrued
Circled the drain, until it was no more

OAKWOOD CEMETERY

When I visited the Fitzgeralds' grave site
A couple years previous
The journey ended on a bittersweet note
Much of what I saw
Were things you'd assume you would see
At the final resting place
Of America's saddest sweethearts
Bottles of gin
Flowers
Gaudy, fake jewels
Photographs and letters
The Fitzgeralds buried in Maryland
It just doesn't work for me
Not because their plot is surrounded
By freeways and suburban strip malls
Not because their graves got dug up
And transferred here
From another local cemetery in the 70s
The main reason
The Rockville gravesite is wrong
Is because it isn't located
In Montgomery Alabama

THE END

AFTERWORD

Although the book is over
The story isn't
Before I sign off
I wanted to share a few more experiences
That happened shortly after my return

The first thing I did when I returned home
Was contact Michael Fedo
To set up an event with him
We booked it at a small art gallery
On West 7th in St. Paul

On my flight home from Montgomery
I began to write
Zelda's Bed
The first draft took five weeks
During this time
The Zelda Fitzgerald fountain was installed
Civic minded people had some kind of hullabaloo
The event was streamed
The fountain is beautiful
The crowd seemed merry

A couple of weeks before Halloween
I went up to Duluth for a few days
One of my highlights was meeting up with my friend
Leif Enger
The wind was blowing 18 mph from the south
We launched kites over Lake Superior
Sometimes we talked
Sometimes we didn't
Later that evening
We went out for pizza with our wives
At the dinner table Leif gifted me the book
Invisible Cities by Italo Calvino
To this day, I've only read half
The story is about an old Kublai Khan
Sitting in a garden and listening to stories
Offered up by a young Marco Polo
Each page is so rich
Each page is a book in itself
I seldom read more than a couple pages at a time
I want to ration my wonder

During this vacation
My wife and I stayed at the Lift Bridge Lodge
The second night of our stay
I pulled out a copy of . . .
The Birds
By British writer Daphne du Maurier
This was the short story
That inspired Alfred Hitchcock's film
I think it was 40 or 42 pages
But pound for pound it was one of the scariest
Books I'd ever read
Actually, we read it out loud to each other
Daphne nailed the ending
To be honest (and my wife will agree)
du Maurier's ending is stronger than Hitchcock's
I was going to read some more of the stories
In the book, but Billy Bama mentioned
He was off to San Francisco
So, I gifted him the book
And he read it at a park
Next to the Golden Gate Bridge

The following afternoon
During a time my wife was napping
I remembered that like Montgomery
Duluth had a monument
Commissioned to honor
The three men lynched
I Googled it and found out
It was less than a mile away
The weather was bleak
But driving someplace
Less than a mile away
Seems like bad form
I decided to walk

The following is an excerpt from my vacation notes . . .
The South by no means has a monopoly
On hate and mistreatment
Hate is Hate
Hate is everywhere
Today I am in Duluth
But I have never seen the memorial
I walked from my hotel, through Canal Park
Across 35 and Superior to First
The trip was 8/10ths of a mile
The majority of my jaunt was within proximity
Of lux restaurants and retail operations
But when I turned onto First
The last 800 feet were overwhelming
Adult bookstores, cannabis shops
Buildings that once possessed success
Were now deserted, dilapidated, hopeless
As I stood at the memorial
Rough people executed daily routines
Most of which I found loud and abrasive
I just stood there trying to process the energy
Past and present
But the only thing that surfaced with clarity
Was confusion

At long last
It was finally time for the Michael Fedo show
As people began to file in
I spotted Michael clad in argyle
His signature look
After introductions and niceties
I commented his sleeves on his sweater were tight
Michael gave me a grin, as he told me modestly
That he was benching 265 lbs. in his early 70s
But then like most weightlifters of a certain age
He blew a shoulder
Next the topic turned to literature
Fedo asked if I had ever heard of Ethel Cline
I said no
Fedo went on to explain . . .

Ethel Cline lived at 599 Summit
The house where Fitzgerald wrote
This Side of Paradise
I was writing columns for different sources
And I thought it might be nice to get a tour
However, there was a sign out front
That said "No Tours"
So, I asked a few people in the know
They told me Ethel advertises no tours
But truth is, there's few things she enjoys
More than showing people around her home
So I made an appointment
I knocked on the door, she cracked it open
I could see she had four chains for security
After I was finally admitted
She had me sign in a guest book
I have to tell you, it was pretty amazing
Just a couple days before me
She toured William Saroyan
I mentioned I didn't know who that was
Fedo seemed surprised, and let me know
You really should read
My Name is Aram
It's a wonderful collection of short stories

Then Fedo guessed . . .
I'm pretty sure you know who John Steinbeck is
I nodded yes
He continued . . .
Steinbeck toured 599 two days before me
I just missed him
Apparently, he was passing through town
While working on his newest project
Travels with Charley
As my eyes bulged out, Fedo pondered . . .
You've got friends at the Historical Society
Somebody, somewhere has to have her register
Wouldn't it be amazing to see all the people
Who toured Fitzgerald's home

40 people plus or minus
Took their seats
I had the honor of discussing
How Michael Feco had impacted me
How his work has taught me
To stop talking to consumers
And start talking to citizens

For 60 minutes, Michael Fedo
In a nutshell told us a story of how
An entire city, terrorized and killed three men
Then tried to erase the episode
As Michael grew deeper into his set
His voice softened, his forehead furrowed
I began to wonder
About the toll he had to endure
Next, I looked at the seated bodies of the audience
For the first 45 minutes, their bodies were stiff
Tense, unsure of what they were supposed to do
Or how they were supposed to react
Then something interesting happened
Without saying it, Fedo basically expressed
He didn't have the answers
He spoke of the murder of George Floyd
Once again, he didn't try to resolve that calamity
But those of us in the audience could see
It was beyond obvious
Michael Fedo encouraged tolerance and kindness
Sometimes readings confuse me
They aren't mathematic, the answers aren't absolute
But on this night, I didn't need an answer
I just felt good being with Michael

That's it friends, I'm out of here
However . . .
I sincerely hope you will exercise ambition
And find a way to order Michael Fedo's
The Lynchings in Duluth
It changed my life, and brought me to a peace
I didn't know existed
Thanks for reading my book
My name is Klecko
Good night!

AUTHOR BIO

Since his last book, Klecko has switched from vodka to whiskey and totaled his Jetta hitting a buck on Highway 61.

The Dead Fitzgeralds
(Book One in Klecko's Fitzgerald Trilogy)

The Dead Fitzgeralds is both poetry and memoir; it's a reflection on the literary legacy of Saint Paul, set against the story of a Baker and his loving friendship with the Poet Laureate of the city, the "Duchess," who became his mentor.

Inspired by the life and work of F. Scott Fitzgerald, who wrote *This Side of Paradise* in a Summit Avenue brownstone catty-corner from the mansion where the Baker lives, he is intent on tapping into the power of a "green light" and becoming the writer he has always wanted to be. As the Duchess slowly faces dementia, she and the Baker become the toast of the literary scene in Saint Paul.

Her guidance leads the Baker toward a deeper appreciation for Scott and Zelda Fitzgerald, and for his city. And after the death of the Duchess, which occurs during the pandemic, he fulfills his destiny as a writer in many ways, ultimately traveling to the Fitzgeralds' gravesite in Rockville, Maryland.

Not only does *The Dead Fitzgeralds* tell a story of deep friendship, loss, literature, and a changing city, but it closes with an element of mysticism on the centennial anniversary of Scott and Zelda's Bad Luck Ball in Saint Paul, and the revelation of Klecko's exclusive Siberian System for tarot.

Does he communicate with Scott Fitzgerald? You'll have to read the book to find out.

www.ingramcontent.com/pod-product-compliance
Lightning Source LLC
Chambersburg PA
CBHW020357130626
46549CB00006B/2320